# Moley's Feasts and Treats

## a seasonal cookbook

# Hannah Giffard

**M**

Pan Macmillan Children's Books

To all those who helped test the recipes
at Hempnall First School,
Leanne, Victoria and Verity,
Daisy, Luke and Jo.
With many thanks.

First published in Great Britain 1994 by
PAN MACMILLAN CHILDREN'S BOOKS
A division of Pan Macmillan Limited
Cavaye Place London SW10 9PG and Basingstoke
Associated companies throughout the world

ISBN 0 333 55842 1

Printed in Hong Kong

# Contents

# Moley's Handy Hints

## Chopping onions

To stop your eyes streaming with tears, keep a piece of bread in your mouth! Try not to swallow it.

## Testing a cake

Take the cake out of the oven. Put a skewer in the top and push through to the bottom. When you take it out, if the skewer has sticky uncooked mixture on it, the cake is <u>not</u> cooked. If the skewer is clean the cake is ready!

## Testing bread

Take the bread out of the oven. Wearing an oven glove, pick up the bread and tap the bottom. If it sounds hollow, it is baked.

A kitchen can be DANGEROUS! So remember these rules:

1. Always have a grown-up to help you with the cooker. Don't ever try to switch the cooker on or off by yourself, or try to open the oven door. ★ When you see this sign always make sure a grown-up is there to help you.

2. ● When you see this sign make sure a grown-up is there to help you with knives and other sharp tools — unless you have special permission. Always cut on a chopping board — NOT on the best table!!

3. If you are allowed to put things in the oven, you must wear a good thick oven glove.
Make sure you only put fireproof dishes in the oven. When you get them out you must put them on a heatproof surface.

4. When cooking on a ring on the top of the cooker, turn pan handles to the sides so that you don't accidentally knock something on the floor.

5. Be extra careful when you are cooking fat, oil, syrup or sugar. If they get too hot they can burn your skin. Turn the heat down if they begin to spit.

Before you start — wash your hands with warm water and soap. Put on a clean apron. Find the utensils you need for your recipe.

Before you finish — the hardest bit...! Wash up all the utensils you've used. Leave the kitchen clean and tidy.

Special Cookery Words... 'to fold' gently and slowly stir the mixture bringing the bottom to the top.
'to rub in' using fingertips break up and 'push' the fat into the flour to form a crumbling mixture.
'separating an egg' tap the egg on top with a knife and make a clean crack. Hold the egg with both hands and gently break in two. Make sure the yolk is in one. Pour the white into a spare saucer. Now pour the yolk into the other half of the egg, letting the white pour out onto the saucer again. Repeat until only the yolk remains.

# VALENTINE'S DAY

## Valentine Heart Biscuits makes 10-15

**Ingredients:**
100g/4oz self-raising flour
50g/2oz softened butter/marg
50g/2oz sugar
2-4 drops vanilla essence
2 tablespoons milk
½ teaspoon cinnamon

**Utensils:**
sieve · wire tray
bowl · jug
wooden spoon
tablespoon
knife or heart-shaped cutter
baking tray

1. Set the oven at 350°F/180°C/Gas 4.

2. Sieve the flour.

3. Rub in the butter until the mixture is crumbly.

4. Add the sugar and stir together.

5. In a separate jug mix 3 drops vanilla with a tbsp. milk.

6. Pour this onto the mixture.

7. Knead the mixture together. If too dry, add extra milk.

8. Sprinkle flour onto the table and roll out the pastry.

9. Cut shapes with a heart-shaped cutter or knife.

10. Place shapes onto a greased baking tray.

11. Bake for 10-15 minutes until a light, golden brown.

12. Cool on a wire tray.

2. Add the lemon juice and beat into a smooth paste.

3. Add the colouring, drop by drop. Mix well until pink.

4. Spread the icing with a wet knife onto biscuit and decorate.

**Biscuit Icing Ingredients:**
oz / 2oz icing sugar
tablespoon lemon juice
ed food colouring – 3 drops
ilver sugar balls

**Utensils:**
sieve · bowl
wooden spoon
knife
tablespoon

1. Sieve the icing sugar into a bowl.

2. Separate the egg. Put yolk aside. Pour white into bowl with the sugar.

3. Mix together adding colour. Then knead until thoroughly blended.

4. Squeeze the lemon. Add juice slowly, until mixture binds together.

# Peppermint Creams

**ngredients:**
100g / 1lb icing sugar
egg · ½ lemon
2 tsp peppermint essence
3 drops red/green
food colouring (optional)

**Utensils:**
2 bowls · sieve
wooden spoon
lemon squeezer
teaspoon
small heart
cutter or knife

5. Add the peppermint essence, drop by drop (½ teaspoon is usually enough!)

6. Press out flat with the palm of your hand. Then cut into hearts.

# MOTHER'S DAY Lemon Drizzle Cake

Ingredients for the cake: 4oz/100g butter
2oz/50g castor sugar · 1 egg · 1 lemon rind
4oz/100g self-raising flour
for the syrup: 2oz/50g castor sugar · 1 lemon

1. Set the oven at 325°C/170°F/gas 3. Melt the butter over a low heat.

2. In a separate bowl beat the egg.

3. Add the castor sugar and butter to the egg and mix.

4. Grate the lemon rind finely. Add flour and fold into mixture

5. Grease a 7" cake tin and pour in the mixture.

6. Bake for 20 minutes in the oven.

7. Make the lemon syrup. Squeeze the juice from the lemon.

8. Pour the juice and sugar into a pan. Stir over low heat until the sugar melts.

9. Turn the cake on to a wire tray to cool.

10. Put it on a plate, prick it with a fork and pour over the syrup.

Utensils:
saucepan · cake tin
lemon squeezer · whisk
wooden spoon · bowl
plate · wire tray

# Chocolate Truffles

**Ingredients:** 6 oz / 150g icing sugar
4 oz / 100g softened butter
1 tablespoon cocoa powder · cream
sprinkles or chocolate powder

Place the softened butter in a bowl.

2. Add the icing sugar and cream until fluffy.

3. Add cocoa. Mix together.

4. Shape into balls and place on a tray.

5. Roll in chocolate powder, or sprinkles, on a plate.

6. Place on a clean plate and leave in fridge for 1 hour.

**Utensils:**
1 bowl
wooden spoon
baking tray
2 plates

# EASTER Pancakes

makes 12-14 pancakes

**Ingredients:**
100g/4oz plain flour
275 ml/10 fl.oz milk
2 teaspoons sunflower oil
a knob of butter
pinch of salt

**Utensils:**
sieve
mixing bowl
hand whisk/electric
wooden spoon
frying pan
fish slice/spatula
small saucer
tablespoon

1. Sift flour into a bowl.

2. Make a well in centre. Add egg and ½ the milk.

3. Whisk gently, bringing in flour from edges. Add rest of milk and whisk.

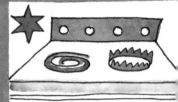

4. Turn on the heat.

5. Put knob of butter in frying pan and melt.

6. Pour off excess butter into saucer, leaving enough just to coat pan.

7. Whisk mixture again and drop 2 tablespoons into the frying pan.

8. Tip pan from side to side to cover the bottom with the batter.

9. Cook quickly, shaking the pan to stop mixture sticking, until the underside is golden.

10. Turn with the fish slice and cook the other side.

11. Now sprinkle with the filling of your choice and roll up.

12. Repeat until finished. Each time add a little more butter to the pan.

## Fillings: Cheese

Grate cheese on to pancake and roll.

## Lemon and sugar

Sprinkle with sugar all over. Then squeeze the lemon juice on top. Roll.

## Chocolate

Melt chocolate in a bowl over hot water. Pour on to pancake and roll.

# EASTER
## Easter Nests

Ingredients:
Nests:
4oz/100g chocolate
2oz/50g cornflakes or puffed ric•

Eggs:
1 block of white marzipan
red and blue food colouring
teaspoon water

Utensils:
saucepan · 2 bowls
wooden spoon · teaspoon
paper cake cases
baking tray · 2 egg cups
clean paintbrush

1. Melt the chocolate over a saucepan of water.

2. Put the cornflakes in a bowl.

3. Pour the chocolate over the cornflakes and stir.

4. Place mixture into paper cases and shape into a nest.

5. Place the nests on a tray.

6. Put this in the fridge to harden.

7. Roll small lumps of marzipan into egg shapes.

8. Mix ½ tsp. of colouring in an egg cup with 1 tsp. of water. Paint on eggs.

9. Remove nests from fridge. Put eggs inside.

# BIRTHDAY TEA
# Flapjacks

**Ingredients:**
75g/3oz brown sugar
150g/6oz butter/margarine
2 tablespoons golden syrup
1 tablespoon honey
250g/10oz porridge oats
75g/3oz coconut

**Utensils:**
saucepan
wooden spoon
8oz square baking

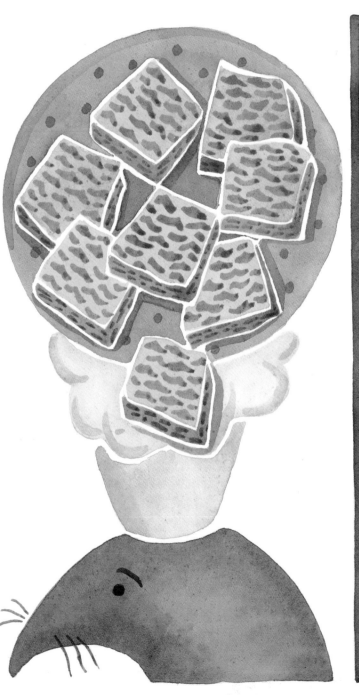

1. Set the oven at 450°F/220°C/Gas 8.

2. Mix sugar, butter, golden syrup and honey together in saucepan until melted.

3. Now add the coconut and porridge oats. Stir until mixed.

4. Press into an 8" square baking tin.

5. Bake in oven for 10-15 minutes until golden brown.

6. Cut into slices while still hot. Leave to cool in tin. Cut flapjacks into 2" squares.

# Sandwich Boats

makes 4 sandwich boats

**Ingredients:**
2 slices of brown bread
25g/1 oz softened butter
50g/2 oz cream cheese
  or margarine
2 slices of cucumber

**Utensils:**
knife for spreading
plate
4 cocktail sticks
sharp knife

1. Spread butter thinly on each slice of bread.

2. Spread the cheese on to one slice. Place the other slice on top.

3. Cut the crusts off carefully around the edges.

4. Cut the sandwich diagonally across into 4 triangles.

5. Slice the cucumber 3mm thick. Cut each slice in half.

6. Pierce with cocktail stick to make sail.

# SUMMER BARBECUE
## Sausage and Bacon Kebabs

**For vegetarians:** Tofu chunks, brushed with soya sauce, or fresh tuna in chunks

Ingredients for each person:
1 sausage
2 bacon rashers
2 small onions
2 small tomatoes
3 button mushrooms
¼ green pepper
oil or melted butter

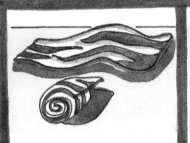

1. Roll up the bacon.

2. Cut the sausages into 3 pieces.

3. Peel the onions, chop tomatoes and pepper, wipe mushrooms.

4. Thread the skewer bacon, onion, tomato, sausage, mushroom etc.

5. Brush with melted butter or oil.

6. Place on the grill. Turn when sides are cooked.

7. For vegetarians: Cut the tofu or tuna into chunks.

Utensils: 1 long or 2 short skewers · small saucepan sharp knife · chopping board · pastry brush

# Avocado and Cheese Salad

Ingredients for 2 people:

avocado · 2 tomatoes · 1 spring onion
lettuce (iceberg or cos) · 50 g / 2 oz cheese
spring onion / 2 sprigs parsley

The dressing:
3 tablespoons vegetable oil
1 teaspoon wine vinegar
pinch salt · pinch pepper
1 teaspoon soy sauce (optional)

Utensils:
sharp knife · chopping board
salad bowl · jam jar with lid !
teatowel

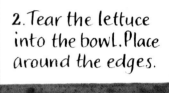

1. Wash and dry the lettuce.

2. Tear the lettuce into the bowl. Place around the edges.

3. Cut the tomatoes and place on top.

4. Cut the avocado. Remove the stone, peel and cut into slices. Place on top.

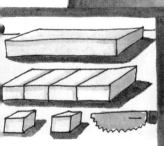

5. Cut the cheese into cubes.

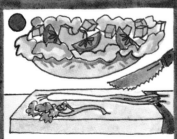

6. Add chopped spring onion and parsley.

7. The dressing: place all the ingredients in the jar and shake.

8. Pour on dressing.

# SUMMER BARBECUE Lemon Cheesecake

## Ingredients:

Base: 200g/8oz digestive biscuits
50g/2oz butter

Filling: 140g/3oz lemon jelly (½ pkt.)
250g/10oz soft cream cheese
2 tablespoons caster sugar
1 large lemon
extra lemon slices and grapes
to decorate

## Utensils:

large saucepan · rolling pin
plastic bag · grater
20cm/8" flan case or deep tin with removable s
bowl · wooden spoon
scissors · measuring jug
lemon squeezer · saucer

1. Cut up jelly, put into jug and pour on the boiling water. Stir well until melted.

2. Cool a little and put in a fridge or freezer.

3. Place biscuits in a plastic bag. Hold closed and crush with rolling pin.

4. Melt butter in a saucepan. Turn off heat. Add crushed biscuits. Mix well.

5. Press into flan ring or tin.

6. Grate lemon rind and squeeze lemon juice.

7. Stir sugar, lemon rind and juice into bowl. Add cream cheese. Beat together.

8. Collect jelly. Beat gradually into mixture. Pour over biscuit base. Refrigerate for 2 hrs.

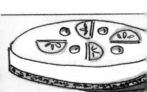

9. When ready tak sides off tin and decorate with 1/2 grapes and lemon slices.

# Moley's Marvellous Milkshakes
## makes one glass

**Ingredients:**
200ml / 7 fl.oz. milk
1 large scoop ice cream
1 small banana or 100g / 4oz strawberries

**Utensils:**
measuring jug
liquidiser
large glass
2 straws

1. Measure 200ml/ 7 fl.oz. milk in measuring jug.

2. Now pour into liquidiser. Add ice cream and either banana or strawberries.

3. Liquidise for 10 seconds. Pour into glass. Add straws.

# Moley's Fruity Cup
## makes one large glass

**Ingredients:**
150 ml / 5 fl.oz. orange juice
90 ml / 3 fl.oz. fizzy water
2 strawberries
2 slices orange
3 ice cubes

**Utensils:**
measuring jug
Sharp knife
1 large glass
2 straws

1. Measure orange juice. Pour into a long glass.

2. Measure fizzy water and add to orange juice.

3. Cut the strawberries. Add ice-cubes and orange slices to the drink.

4. Pop the straws in and enjoy Moley's fruit cup!

# HARVEST FESTIVAL Harvest Bread

## Ingredients:
300g / 12 oz flour · pinch of salt
½ sachet quick-action dried yeast
1 dessertspoon veg./sunflower oil
210 ml / ⅜ pint warm water

## The Glaze:
1 egg
¼ teaspoon water

## Utensils:
Large bowl · fork
baking tray
measuring jug
cup · wire tray
sieve · spoon

1. Set the oven at 425° F / 220° C / gas 7.

2. Sieve the flour. Add yeast and salt.

3. Make a well. Add oil and warm water. Mix into firm dough.

4. If too dry, add water. If too wet, add more flour.

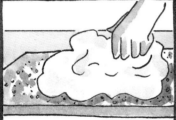

5. Put dough on floured surface. Knead well. Make plait or wheatsheaf.

6. Glaze Separate egg. Keep yolk; beat with ¼ teaspoon water. Brush on top.

7. Place on greased baking tray. Bake for 15-20 minutes until golden brown.

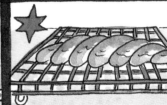

8. Tap bottom for hollow sound. Cool on a wire tray.

# The Plait

    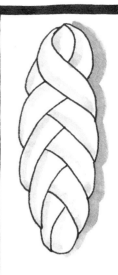

Make 3 long ugh sausages. nt ends with ze. Press together.

2. Follow the drawing. Bring right sausage to centre.

3. Now left to centre.

4. Then right to centre again. Continue to end.

5. Now stick sausages down again with glaze.

# The Wheatsheaf

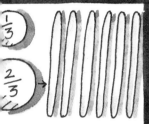

Divide dough into and ⅔ balls. ke ⅔ and form nto 6 sausages.

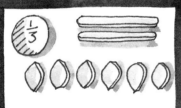

2. Now use other ⅓. Make 6 leaf shapes and 2 thin sausages.

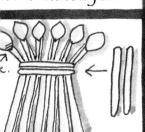

Stick leaf shapes to ends with egg aze. Then stick sausages.

4. Use knife to make wheat imprint.

# THANKSGIVING Pecan Pie

**Ingredients for base:**
150g/6oz plain flour
75g/3oz margarine
4 tablespoons cold water

**Ingredients for filling:**
4 large eggs
225g/8oz real maple syrup
few squirts fresh lemon juice
½ teaspoon cinnamon
25g/1oz butter (melted)
½ teaspoon vanilla essence
100g/4oz pecans or walnuts
(save 4 for decoration)

**Utensils:**
electric mixer
saucepan
sieve
round-edged knife
tablespoon
2 bowls
9" pie dish
rolling pin

1. Set oven at 375°F/ 190°C/ Gas 5.

2. Sieve the flour into the bowl.

3. Cut cubes of margarine into flour, rub in until crumbly.

4. Sprinkle 4 tablesp. water over mixture; use knife to mix.

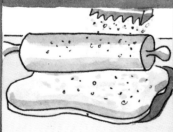

5. Add more water if too dry. Sprinkle flour over surface, and roll flat.

6. Lightly roll pastry round pin and transfer to greased pie dish.

7. Press down into edges with fingers; trim edges with knife.

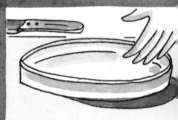

8. Put in cool place. Now make filling.

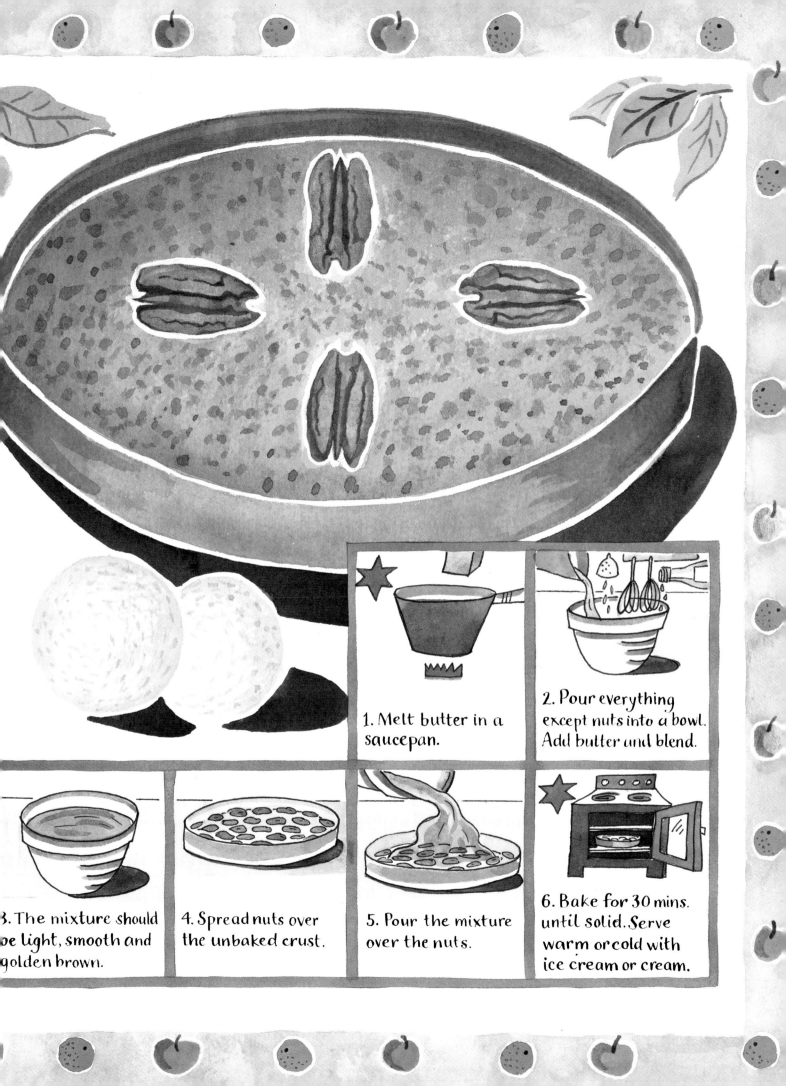

1. Melt butter in a saucepan.

2. Pour everything except nuts into a bowl. Add butter and blend.

3. The mixture should be light, smooth and golden brown.

4. Spread nuts over the unbaked crust.

5. Pour the mixture over the nuts.

6. Bake for 30 mins. until solid. Serve warm or cold with ice cream or cream.

# HALLOWE'EN Pumpkin Cookies

## Ingredients:
200 g / 8 oz sugar · 100 g / 4 oz margarine · 1 egg
200 g / 8 oz pumpkin flesh · 200 g / 8 oz flour · pinch of salt
½ teacup chopped walnuts and raisins
2 teaspoons cinnamon · 1 teaspoon vanilla essence
1 teaspoon baking           1 teaspoon bicarb.
   powder                     of soda

## Utensils:
baking tray
bowl
wooden spoon
chopping board
sharp knife
metal spatula / fish slice
wire tray

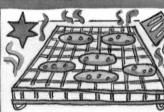

1. Set the oven at 375° F / 190°C / Gas 5.

2. Cut off pumpkin skin and chop flesh into small cubes.

3. Mix all ingredients together in bowl with wooden spoon.

4. Place drops of mixture 4-5 cm across on greased baking tray.

5. Bake 8-10 minutes Remove and cool on wire tray.

# Toffee Apples

**Ingredients:**
6 apples
25g/1oz butter
100g/4oz golden syrup
25g/1oz sugar
juice of ½ lemon

**Utensils:**
small lengths of thin
dowelling/6 lollipop sticks
heavy-bottomed saucepan
bowl of cold water
greaseproof paper
baking tray
wooden spoon

1. Remove stems and push sticks into top of apple until firm.

2. Heat butter, syrup, sugar and lemon juice together in saucepan. Mix well.

3. Boil and stir until golden brown. Do not let bottom burn.

4. Turn heat right down. Dip apples into toffee and twist round.

5. Dip into cold water for 1 minute to harden toffee. Lay out on greaseproof paper.

# HANNUKKAH Potato Latkes

**Ingredients:**
4 large potatoes
2 eggs
4 level teaspoons self-raising flour
salt to taste
pinch of pepper
grated onion, optional

**Utensils:**
grater · potato peeler
2 bowls · sieve
frying pan
spatula
fish slice

1. Peel the potatoes.

2. Grate potatoes finely into a pulp.

3. Transfer to a colander and press out liquid. Drain for 10-15 minutes.

4. Put all ingredients together in a bowl and mix.

5. Flatten mixture into a patty.

6. Heat 1" oil in frying pan. To test add 1 teaspoon mixture.

7. Cook for 4-5 minutes either side on a steady heat until a rich brown.

8. Drain and eat immediately.

# CHRISTMAS Moley's Christmas Log

**Ingredients:**
30 ml/2 tablespoons milk
50 g/2 oz butter
200 g/7 oz icing sugar
20 g/2 tablespoons cocoa powder
1 bar plain chocolate
1 ready-made chocolate cake roll
holly for decoration

**Utensils:**
saucepan · wooden spoon
sieve · bowl · large plate
grater · measuring jug
palette knife · tablespoon

1. Sieve together icing sugar and cocoa.

2. Heat the milk and butter together until melted.

3. Pour butter mixture into cocoa and sugar. Beat together until smooth and creamy.

4. Leave to cool for 10 minutes.

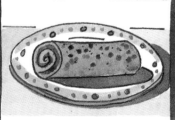
5. Take cake out of packet and place on a large plate.

6. Now spread icing generously onto the roll with a wet palette knife.

7. Grate chocolate all over the icing.

8. Leave in a cool place to harden icing. Decorate with holly.

# CHRISTMAS Chocolate Leaves

 1. Melt the chocolate in a bowl over a saucepan of hot water.

 2. Dip a leaf (veined side up) in the chocolate.

 3. Remove and put the leaf, chocolate side up, on a plate.

 4. Put the leaves in the fridge for ½ hour.

 5. Peel the leaf from the back of the chocolate.

Ingredients: 1 block plain or milk chocolate · selection of washed holly or rose leaves

Utensils: saucepan · bowl large plate wooden spoon

## Sticky Toffee

Utensils: heavy saucepan wooden spoon · tablespoon teaspoon · 7" tin (buttered)

Ingredients:
75g/3oz butter
1 tin condensed milk
2 tablespoons golden syrup · 1 teaspoon vanilla essence

 1. Put the butter, condensed milk and syrup in a saucepan.

 2. Bring to the boil and then stir for 17 minutes.

 3. Take off heat and stir in 1 teaspoon vanilla essence.

 4. Turn into tin, mark into squares and cool.

# Crumbly Chocolate Fudge

1. Put the biscuits in a plastic bag. Hold closed and crush.

2. Melt the chocolate and butter in bowl over hot water.

3. Stir in the syrup, biscuit crumbs and almonds.

4. Place the mixture in the tin, press down flat.

5. Leave to set for 1 hour.

6. Cut into large cubes, remove gently.

Ingredients:
2 tablespoons golden syrup
50g/2oz butter
100g/4oz plain chocolate
125g/5oz sweet biscuits
25g/1oz ground almonds

Utensils:
rolling pin
plastic bag
bowl · knife
wooden spoon
saucepan
7" square tin (buttered)

# CHRISTMAS Apricot Snowballs

## Ingredients:
100g/4oz dried apricots · 2 teaspoons honey
65g/2½oz mixed nuts · 1 orange · 2 teasp. orange juice
dried coconut _or_ hazelnuts and almonds to decorate

## Utensils:
2 bowls · colander
liquidizer · grater
orange squeezer
teaspoon · wooden spo[on]
board

1. Place apricots in bowl. Cover with boiling water and soak for 5 minutes.

2. In a separate bowl, finely grate the orange and lemon rind.

3. Squeeze the orange; add 2 teaspoons of juice to rind.

4. Place nuts in liquidiser; chop fine[ly] and add to rind.

5. Drain apricots and liquidise for 1-2 minutes.

6. Put the mixture into the bowl. Beat with 2 teaspoons of honey. Knead well.

7. Roll into balls.

8. Roll in coconut or press a whole nu[t] into the ball.